David Said, "The Lord Is My Shepherd." Who Is Your Shepherd?

The Fourth Letter of Apostle Andy From God to the Joshua Generation of 2022

Written By
Apostle Andrew Giannelli

Charleston, South Carolina

AG Production
Charleston, SC 29461
odm@homesc.com
Printed in the United States of America First Printing, 2022

This Book Belongs To

Date

____

Thank you for your support

PREFACE

When I minister, the Holy Spirit brings examples to help explain biblical truths. It may appear as if I am going down rabbit's trails but at the end it will bring clarity. I write the way I minister.

PRAYER:

And so, from the day we heard, we have not ceased to pray for you, asking that you may be filled with the knowledge of his will in all spiritual wisdom and understanding, [10] so as to walk in a manner worthy of the Lord, fully pleasing to him: bearing fruit in every good work and increasing in the knowledge of God; [11]being strengthened with all power, according to his glorious might, for all endurance and patience with joy; [12] giving thanks to the Father, who has qualified you to share in the inheritance of the saints in light. **Colossians 1:9-12 ESV**

Apostle Andy to the Saints of the Joshua generation who are also faithful to God. Apostle Andrew Giannelli

Psalm 23 RSV
The Divine Shepherd
A Psalm of David.

The LORD is my shepherd, I shall not want; 2he makes me lie down in green pastures. He leads me beside still waters; [Heb the waters of rest] 3he restores my soul, [Or life] He leads me in paths of righteousness {Or right paths} for his name's sake.

4 Even though I walk through the valley of the shadow of death, [Or the valley of deep darkness] I fear no evil; for thou art with me; thy rod and thy staff, they comfort me. 5Thou preparest a table before me in the presence of my enemies; thou anointest my head with oil, my cup overflows. 6 Surely [Or Only] goodness and mercy [Or kindness] shall follow me all the days of my life; and I shall dwell in the house of the LORD forever. [Or as long as I live]

John 21:15 TLB

After breakfast Jesus said to Simon Peter, "Simon, son of John, do you love me more than these others? "Yes," Peter replied, "you know I am your friend." "Then feed my lambs," Jesus told him.

Feed here means exactly what a shepherd did back then he grazed or pastured the sheep. To do this they were to get them to God's pasture not a man. To get them to be taught by the Comforter.

1 John 2:27 AMP

As for you, the anointing [the special gift, the preparation] which you received from Him remains [permanently] in you, and you have no need for anyone to teach you. But just as His anointing teaches you [giving you insight through the presence of the Holy Spirit] about all things, and is true and is not a lie, and just as His anointing has taught you, you must remain in Him [being rooted in Him, knit to Him].

John 21:16 TLB

Jesus repeated the question:"Simon, son of John, do you really love me?" "Yes, Lord," Peter said, "you know I am your friend." "Then take care of my sheep," Jesus said.

This means watch over them. So, I refer to the above scripture. Watch over means protect from those who would wrongfully manipulate the sheep. Those who would try to become there leader instead of getting them to God as their father. Did not Jesus instruct them and us to pray Our Father who art in heaven? Well, He either is your Father, or He is not.

If He, that is God, is your Father as He was Jesus's father, and David's shepherd why are you letting someone else direct you? He sent the Comforter that you have need that no man teaches you. Quit letting someone other than God be your Father, or head, or shepherd.

You have not had all the gifts [ministers] that God sent to you by Jesus working on your behalf to build you up for God, but they have been mostly manipulating God's sheep. Most ministers' primary purpose has not been to do what God had Jesus send them to do for you as a gift to you. Their primary purpose from God is to build you up for God's purpose, and what God anointed you to do for God and the body. They have neglected their purpose for God for the saints. God is raising up for Himself a

Joshua generation and Joshua leaders to take the land God has for them. He started training me as a Joshua generation leader, for this generation, forty years ago.

John 21:17 TLB

Once more he asked him, "Simon, son of John, are you even my friend?" Peter was grieved at the way Jesus asked the question this third time. "Lord, you know my heart; you know I am," he said. Jesus said, "Then feed my little sheep.

This feed here is the same as the first one, pasture or graze in God's pasture. David wrote this Psalm after he killed Goliath. He was placing himself as a sheep of God's pasture. Even though God used him to slay Goliath, he didn't get prideful like some others today or those in the Bible when God used them. His relationship with the sheep as a shepherd, caused him to understand the relationship he had with God as his shepherd watching over him, which gave him the confidence to stand against Goliath for God. David understood that God was his shepherd and would protect him just as God anointed him to protect the sheep he watched over for his father. Today, many ministers who are used by God get lifted up, or shall I say exalted above the sheep, like they are "something", rather than a gift from God to the sheep.

Matthew 18:12 AMP

What do you think? If a man has a hundred sheep, and one of them gets lost, will he not leave the ninety-nine on the mountain and go in search of the one that is lost? 13 And if it turns out that he finds it, I assure you and most solemnly say to you, he rejoices over it more than over the ninety-nine that did not get lost.

14 So it is not the will of your Father who is in heaven that one of these little ones be lost.

You see, a true shepherd goes after a lost sheep. Some sheep get cast down and cannot get back up. They need someone to help them stand up again. A cast sheep is a sheep that has laid down and can't get up because its center of gravity is off – sometimes because it's pregnant or simply because it has a full fleece. When the fleece is full it gets dirty and heavy and some-times when they lay down, especially if they are wet from the rain, they cannot get up. Once the sheep is cast down, gasses start to build up in its abdomen and it can die in a matter of hours. If you get it back up on its feet, then it's fine.

A lady called my wife and asked to borrow twenty dollars for a few days. God told my wife no, but when she and I prayed, God said just give her forty as a gift. You see, her husband left her with some small children one just over one year old. That night me, my wife, and our 8 children living at home, prayed about what to do. God told one of my children to give thirty dollars, another to give fifty dollars, and me to give five hundred dollars. When we gave her the money the next morning, we found out she had no food in the house and did not get paid till Thursday.

You see, she was cast down. I told her God said several people knew your situation but would not help, including the church she was going to. I considered her a widow with children and no husband helping.

How many leaders would never leave their office to go to a sheep in trouble? They will not leave the ninety-nine to go for the one cast down. Matthew 25 talks about that judgement day coming. They do not have the heart of God, and they are not true shepherds after God's own heart.

John 10:27-31 NIV

My sheep listen to my voice, and I know them, and they follow me. 28 I give them eternal life, and they will never perish; no one will snatch them from my hand. 29 My Father, who has given them to me, is greater than all, and no one can snatch them from my Father's hand. 30 The Father and I are one." 31 The Jewish leaders picked up rocks again to stone him to death.

Man cannot teach you Gods voice, but the comforter will. Ask the Lord to be your shepherd and quit listening to fleshly ministers who are manipulating you for their purpose. If you get cast down, you will not be able to count on them. They will just leave you to die.

The Judgment
Matthew 25:31-46 NET

When the Son of Man comes in his glory and all the angels with him, then he will sit on his glorious throne. 32 All the nations will be assembled before him, and he will separate people one from another like a shepherd separates the sheep from the goats. 33 He[ah] will put the sheep on his right and the goats on his left. 34 Then the king will say to those on his right, 'Come, you who are blessed by my Father, inherit the kingdom prepared for you from the foundation of the world. 35 For I was hungry and you gave me food, I was thirsty and you gave me something to drink, I was a stranger and you invited me in, 36 I was naked and you gave me clothing, I was sick and you took care of me, I was in prison and you visited me.' 37 Then the righteous will answer him, 'Lord, when did we see you hungry and feed you, or thirsty and give you something to drink? 38 When did we see you a stranger and invite you in, or naked and clothe you? 39 When did we see you sick or in prison and visit you?' 40 And the king will answer them, 'I tell you the truth, just as you did it for one of the least of these brothers or sisters of mine, you did it for me.'

41 "Then he will say to those on his left, 'Depart from me, you accursed, into the eternal fire that has been prepared for the devil and his angels! 42 For I was hungry and you gave me nothing to eat, I was thirsty and you gave me nothing to drink. 43 I was a stranger and you did not receive me as a guest, naked and you did not clothe me, sick and in prison and you did not visit me.' 44 Then they too will answer, 'Lord, when did we see you hungry

or thirsty or a stranger or naked or sick or in prison, and did not give you whatever you needed?' 45 Then he will answer them, 'I tell you the truth, just as you did not do it for one of the least of these, you did not do it for me.' 46 And these will depart into eternal punishment, but the righteous into eternal life."*

Ezekiel 16:49 AMP

Behold, this was the sin of your sister Sodom: she and her daughters (outlying cities) had arrogance [pride], abundant food, and careless ease, but she did not help the poor and needy. 50 They were haughty and committed repulsive acts before Me; therefore, I removed them when I saw it.

The repulsive things were homosexuals which most everyone talks about, but I do not hear ministers talking about the fact that they were not helping the poor and needy. The needy and poor were listed before the homosexuals. The people crying out from Sodom were the needy, but still, none of them were righteous.

Mark 7:6 AMP

He replied, "Rightly did Isaiah prophesy about you hypocrites (play-actors, pretenders), as it is written [in Scripture],

'THESE PEOPLE HONOR ME WITH THEIR LIPS, BUT THEIR HEART IS FAR FROM ME. 7 'THEY WORSHIP ME IN VAIN [their worship is meaningless and worthless, a pretense], TEACHING THE PRECEPTS OF MEN AS DOCTRINES [giving their traditions equal weight with the Scriptures].'

Here, Jesus is talking to the Pharisees and some of the scribes of that day, and to some of the leaders of today also. Just like today their way of doing things, especially in church services, are their habits or tradition and are given greater weight then what God wants done in the services according to the scriptures and the Spirit. Read 1 Corinthians 14:26-33 RSV

Orderly Worship

26 What then, brethren? When you come together, each one has a hymn, a lesson, a revelation, a tongue, or an interpretation. Let all things be done for edification. "When you come together" back then was mostly in houses. Study when they first started meetings in a bigger building.

27 If any speak in a tongue, let there be only two or at most three, and each in turn; and let one interpret. 28 But if there is no one to interpret, let each of them keep silence in church and speak to himself and to God. Now here is something I have never seen done in a church service. It is always one man speaking, especially prophesying.

29 Let two or three prophets speak, and let the others weigh what is said.

Why would the word say weigh (judge) what is being said unless some things said would not be of God or correct?

30 If a revelation is made to another sitting by, let the first be silent.

To do this, you would have to get a word of knowledge that God gave someone else a word. One night while doing a street meeting in the Dominican Republic, God told me I did not have the message for that night. I asked, "Who has the message?" The apostle's wife in that town raised her hand. She was outstanding with the message she brought. Then she told everyone her husband, the apostle, told her to prepare to bring a message that night because God wanted her to minister that night. She had never preached before. That's what you call being led by the Spirit and doing it God's way. You see God chose to have her minister that night, not me.

31 For you can all prophesy one by one, so that all may learn, and all be encouraged.

The scripture says you can all prophesy one by one. The capability for all to prophecy was poured out in the upper room on the day of Pentecost over 2,000 years ago, but I do not know the last time in over 2,000 years this was done by any ministers or allowed in the congregation. They keep their tradition of a one man show and of everyone singing for half a service, and in some places even more. That is a tradition not led by the Spirit. Most say they are preparing the atmosphere. I have never read that in the Bible or been instructed by the Spirit to do this. I have had services where God had given as many as 14 new songs to 14 different people in one service, songs that they never heard before but were given by the Spirit. In all the times Jesus spoke in the Bible I do not know of one time Jesus said or instructed let's sing some songs first then I will teach or preach or pray for you. Yet I do not see any services today that they do not sing first. Singing is given priority over the word and ministry. They are not being led by the Spirit.

32 and the spirits of prophets are subject to prophets. 33 For God is not a God of confusion but of peace.

This means if the prophets do not speak two or three and what they are saying is judged, there will be confusion and that is why there is so much confusion today. There is no judging what is said and done. Most prophets tell the people, "I do not hear enough Amens!" and then ask for them to be louder. Then one of the things they say is, "If you love the Lord stand up and shout, give Him a wave offering, clap offering!" and so on. Did Jesus ever ask for Amens and have all the people stand up and shout like most ministers today? Did Jesus dim the lights to create an atmosphere, and have praise and worship to the Father so He could minister better? It is called tradition. The church has gotten into manipulating the saints and trying to be like the world. When you are being led by the Spirit of God, there is no male or female in the Spirit.

Most leader are cheerleaders getting the people to cheer and get stirred up for God. They have no idea how many real Christians that follow God they run off. Of course, that is the goal of the flesh to be seen and lifted up by the people not God They stir people up with instruments and singing rather than obeying

God and letting the Spirit stir them up in their Spirit and build the people up in their Spirit.

1 Samuel 17:31-37 RSV

When the words which David spoke were heard, they repeated them before Saul; and he sent for him. 32 And David said to Saul, "Let no man's heart fail because of him; your servant will go and fight with this Philistine." 33 And Saul said to David, "You are not able to go against this Philistine to fight with him; for you are but a youth, and he has been a man of war from his youth."

34 But David said to Saul, "Your servant used to keep sheep for his father; and when there came a lion, or a bear, and took a lamb from the flock, 35 I went after him and smote him and delivered it out of his mouth; and if he arose against me, I caught him by his beard, and smote him and killed him. 36 Your servant has killed both lions and bears; and this uncircumcised Philistine shall be like one of them, seeing he has defied the armies of the living God." 37 And David said, "The LORD who delivered me from the paw of the lion and from the paw of the bear, will deliver me from the hand of this Philistine." And Saul said to David, "Go, and the LORD be with you!

You see here in this passage; David gave God all the glory. Remember, he was a Shepherd over his father's sheep, and now he is comparing himself as a sheep to the Lord in Psalm 23. David took a position as a shepherd before the army and protected the whole army, including the king. What position are you taking as a minister? Are you protecting the sheep or using them for your purpose? If you're a sheep, are you being manipulated by a person instead of being taught to be led by God and become a David in God's flock? Even though he slayed the lion and the bear, then killed the giant, who none of the soldiers or the king would go up against, David still was not up in pride like most people being used by God today. Is the person you're following building you up for what God has anointed you to do? Or are they using you to accomplish their goal? Consider the ass that spoke to Balaam. He went back to serving Balaam after saving Balaam's life.

Many servants today have words from God for who they are serving but, who they are serving are so exalted in themselves, they can't or will not receive the word from a servant. We are all purposed to be servants. The point is, do not get exalted because God chooses to use you. Remember, you are His sheep. If you can see that, then you will realize that the Lord is your shepherd. The ministers are a gift to the sheep from God to build them up for the work of the ministry. If you're under a minister is his primary goal to build you up for God to do what God has anointed you to do, or is he more concerned with what he wants to accomplish?

David came to the revelation as God used him to take care of the sheep, that God was taking care of him as his Shepherd. Have you come to that revelation yet, that God wants to be your shepherd and doesn't want you following a man? Are you submitting to God as your Shepherd, or are you submitting to a man or religion?

The whole army, including the king, were not walking like David was with God. The same is happening today. God has His remanent who are wholly following God. That does not mean others are not following God. They are not fully following, just partially. A lot of leaders are like the king of that day who sought no council from God at all. And the leadership today are like the king was to David in those days.

Verse 33 And Saul said to David, *"You are not able to go against this Philistine to fight with him; for you are but a youth, and he has been a man of war from his youth."*

You can see Saul was a carnal leader, but David was God's man and did not let Saul's word get into his heart. You can say the fiery darts of the flesh did not penetrate David's shield of faith. Do not be amazed when you find out your leader does not know God or walk with God as close as you do. He could have a lot of head knowledge of the word but not know how to be led by the Spirit or walk with God like you do.

The shield of faith and the fiery darts both come from words spoken to you. The shield of faith is what God has told you or taught you by being yoked with God or what He has said to you. Fiery darts are what the enemy or anyone tells you that is not from God. Like here in the scripture above, fiery darts can come from your leader. David did not receive what the king said but what he had heard and experienced by fully following God.

Ministers and people were always telling me you need to be under a pastor, but I knew God told me not to join a church or denomination. God was going to teach me. In other words, God was my shepherd. God was yoking me to Jesus for me to learn from Jesus-not of Jesus but from Him rather than from a man. I will just mention here a church that just has a pastor for a leader that is not working together with an apostle, prophet, evangelist, and teacher is like a single parent momma and will never be able to develop the sheep like God has ordained them to be developed. God said that is the biggest problem in the world today, single parent mammas. God said I send them a good husband, but they will not let the husband be the head and the husbands either submit to the wife or leave. God said it is the same in the churches today. I send my apostles and prophets to the pastors and teachers, but they will not allow them to lead. The prophets and apostles either submit to the pastors instead of Me or leave.

He gave five gifts to the body, not one. If you think you can build up the saints by yourself, it is not of God. The goal you have for your church is yours, not God's. God said He was going to build His church on the foundation of the apostles and prophets, not pastors and teachers. God asked me years ago, what was Jesus? I said

He was a tried stone, a precious corner stone, a sure foundation. God said, "that is right, and I am not putting any junk in My foundation with Him." My apostles and prophets will be tried and tested just like Jesus was. At that time, in 1983, I built big houses. When the foundation man got done laying block, there was scattered all around the foundation busted and cracked block that could not be used in the foundation of the house being built.

Many of these foundations were as high as six feet tall and there were a lot of blocks on the ground; so many, we had to clean them all up just to be able to walk around the house to put in the floor system. God spoke to me one day and said, "these busted blocks, and there were many, are like my apostles and prophets who did not make it into the foundation of the church I am building. They were tried and tested and did not make it. They could not take it when they were tried and tested. They broke or cracked. When it came to dying to themselves like Jesus' drinking God's cup, they could not do it. They could not come to the place where they would say and mean it, "not my will be done but the Father's will be done." They could not, and they cracked or broke under the weight of the command. They will not make it into what God is doing.

Psalm 100:3 KJV

Know ye that the LORD he is God: it is he that hath made us, and not we ourselves; we are his people, and the sheep of his pasture.

Psalm 100:3 AMP

Know and fully recognize with gratitude that the LORD Himself is God; It is He who has made us, not we ourselves [and we are

His]. We are His people and the sheep of His pasture.

Psalms is Old Testament how much more are we today God's sheep and He is our pasture.

So, if the Apostles, Prophets, Evangelist, Pastors and Teachers are not building up the saints as God has ordained them to do, the sheep will never attain to what God wants them to attain to. So, God will take over and do the job Himself or bring in the next generation to do the job this and the last generation would not obey God to do. So, if the ministers will not do what God ordained them to do, what do you think God is going to say or do to them?

Don't sheep eat in a pasture? If so, then why are the pastors feeding the sheep instead of leading them to God's pasture to eat? You will say the pastor feeds them the word, but the pastor does not have a pasture like God does,

does he? Some may say the pastor is receiving from God to give to the sheep, but the Apostle John says that the Holy Spirit will teach you. You can receive directly from God just as the pastor does or says he does. You can be taught by God or man. The choice is yours.

1 John 2:26-27 RSV

I am writing these things to you about those who are trying to lead you astray. 27 but the anointing which you received from him abides in you, and you have no need that anyone should teach you; as his anointing teaches you about everything, and is true, and is no lie, just as it has taught you, abide in him.

That's a word from the Lord's pasture you probably have not gotten from most leaders. God told me if you want to teach something, teach the sheep how to be taught by the Holy Spirit. So, if you're being told to come to church because you need someone to teach you and give you instruction, you are being deprived of being taught by the Spirit of God. You are taught to focus on flesh not Spirit. Many ministers are using the gifts of the Spirit to get you to follow them instead of teaching you to flow in the gifts of the Spirit like them for others. If you sow to the Spirit, you will reap of the Spirit.

I hope you can see that ministers who are not building you up for what God has anointed you to do for God are keeping you from learning to sow in the Spirit and in doing so are also keeping you from reaping from the Spirit. If you reap what you sow and you sow building others up, which the scripture says to earnestly desire to prophecy that you may build others up, how built up can you get because of what you are going to reap? Think about how built up or how big can you get.

In John 16:12 Jesus said *I have more things to teach you, but you cannot handle or bear it now*. In other words, if He told you, it would blow you away in modern terms. Just like in Matthew 16:13-28 when Jesus told Peter what was going to happen to Jesus, and Peter started rebuking Jesus. He could not receive it, and Jesus said get behind me Satan. Jesus went on to say when the comforter or Spirit of truth comes, He will guide you into all the truth. He will only say what He hears. He will not speak on His own authority. He will also tell you things that are to come which are prophecy. He will give me all the glory for He will only give you what I give Him to say. The same way Jesus did His Father. All that the Father has belongs to me and He will take what is mine and reveal it to you when I tell Him to.

Have you or your minister been declared to

be the Spirit of truth by God? Have you been informed that the Spirit of truth will guide you into all truth? Or do you believe or have been told that your leaders will lead you into all truth? Have you been told you need no man to teach you, but the Spirit of God will teach you, or have you been lied to?

Most ministers think they know it all. That is why the Spirit of truth is not showing them anything because Jesus is not telling the Spirit to tell them anything. When a minister gets between you and God, they are eclipsing you from God just as when the moon gets between the earth and the sun. The ministers have no light of their own but reflect the Son [Jesus]. So, if the ministers are getting between you and Jesus, they have no light of their own and are keeping you from getting the light God wants you to receive. Without the sun the plants on earth will not grow. What's going to happen to you if the ministers keep you or block you from the Son?

John 10:1 RSV

Jesus said I Am the Good Shepherd if you do not come in the sheepfold by the door but some other way you are a thief or robber.

But when you enter by the door you are the shepherd. He, the gatekeeper, opens the gate for the shepherd, and the sheep know His voice, He calls them by name, and they follow His lead. When He gets them out, He goes before them, and they know His voice and follow Him. Do you know His voice? He said my sheep know my voice and will not follow another. Who are you following? It says they will flee from a stranger because they do not know a stranger's voice. Do you need to flee from a stranger in your walk with God?

John 10:6-18 RSV

This figure of speech Jesus used with them, but they did not understand what he was saying to them. 7 So Jesus again said to them, "Truly, truly, I say to you, I am the door of the sheep. 8 All who came before me are thieves and robbers, but the sheep did not listen to them. 9 I am the door. If anyone enters by me, he will be saved and will go in and out and find pasture.

10 The thief comes only to steal and kill and destroy. I came that they may have life and have it abundantly. 11 I am the good shepherd. The good shepherd lays down his life for the sheep. 12 He who is a hired hand and not a shepherd, who does not own the sheep, sees the wolf coming and leaves the sheep and flees, and the wolf snatches them and scatters them. 13 He flees because he is a hired hand

and cares nothing for the sheep. 14 I am the good shepherd. I know my own and my own know me, 15 just as the Father knows me and I know the Father; and I lay down my life for the sheep. 16 And I have other sheep that are not of this fold. I must bring them also, and they will listen to my voice. So there will be one flock, one shepherd.

17 For this reason the Father loves me, because I lay down my life that I may take it up again. 18 No one takes it from me, but I lay it down of my own accord. I have authority to lay it down, and I have authority to take it up again. This charge I have received from my Father."

Jesus is talking and says He is your shepherd, not a man or religion. The only thing you need a minister to teach you is how to be taught by the Holy Spirit. That's what the Bible says.

You have need that no man teaches you, but the Comforter will. Jesus said, I have more to show you, but the Comforter will show you. Jesus also said, all that the Father has is mine, and I will reveal it to you by the Spirit, not by a man or denomination, but by God's Spirit.

When I got born again on January 10, 1982, in the Assembly of God, God instantly started speaking to me giving me revelation and using me in the gifts. They saw the call on my life and told me I needed to join the church so they could train me to minister in their denomination. When I went to put the application in the offering plate, God said if I joined the Assembly of God, I would be worse off than I was as a Catholic. In the first letter I wrote, I did not say the denominations names because I did not think it would be right to say their names, but the truth is the truth and that is what God told me, like it or not. God told me He would teach me. God is no respecter of persons. If He will teach me, He will teach you. In other words, He will be my shepherd, and He will be yours too if you want.

God would use me after services some days in different churches, and the pastor would say, "Whoever your pastor is, he is blessed." They would ask me, who is your pastor? I would tell them I just walk with God, and then I was invited not to come back.

A girl by the name of Lynn Brown met me and took me to a shut in at Goodwill AME Church in Mt Pleasant, SC. God used me to minister to some of the people. Then she started taking me to more shut-ins in Mt. Pleasant S.C. All the people that showed up for the shut-ins were women. I was the only man and only white person. In all of the months that we did shut-ins, not one minister ever came, but God was using me to build the people up on how to minister one to another. I didn't know my call then, nor was I in ministry yet, but God was using me to build up the saints for the work of the ministry.

St. Andrews Episcopal Church members had home meetings for Cursillo. People I prayed for were getting filled with the Holy Spirt with speaking in tongues. I was not welcome any more. One day, God told me to go to a Wednesday service at Saint Andrews. I did not want to go. I told God those people do not like me, but I obeyed and went. At the end of the service, I told God if He wanted me to pray for anyone, He would need to bring them to me. I had only been walking with God about a year when all this was happening. This young Methodist boy came up to me and said, "Do you remember the night you prayed for me, and I received the Holy Spirit with the evidence of speaking in tongues? You said someone did not believe what was happening was of God." I said, "Yes". He said, "This girl that is with me is the one that did not believe, and she wants you to pray for her." This girl was around fifteen years old.

We went to the alter, and she knelt down. No one touched her. When I prayed for her, she jumped off the alter praying in tongues. She said she saw a bright light come down on her and hit her belly, and she started speaking in tongues. I told her to kneel back down, and as I was praying over her in tongues, she jumped up and said, "I know what you're saying!" I ask her what I was saying, and she said, "The wolf is coming! The wolf is coming!" The priest came walking in the sanctuary. I had told her not to tell her parents unless God told her to since they probably would not understand because of the denomination they were in. She asked, "Can I tell the priest?" and she did. The next day I got a phone call from the assistant priest telling me not to come back or pray for anybody at their church.

The priest's name if I remember was John Bucannon and Jack Knighter was the assistant. I am mentioning names because these are the wolves in sheep's clothing leading many astray and are not open to the Holy Spirit. What is going on against God in most churches is real, but most will not say it or confront those anti-Christ leaders. They are anti- the move of the Spirit, but God is raising up a Joshua generation to take back the land that belongs to God's people.

I have many more testimonies, but what I

wanted you to see is that God was my shepherd at a very young age in the Lord. Shortly after my walk with God started, I was driving down the highway and saw a dump truck loaded with dirt with 4 cars following it on a 4-lane high-way not even doing the speed limit. As I passed them, I said to myself, "Why don't they pass the truck?" God spoke to me and said, "They are like a lot of my people. They are following a loaded down pastor and cannot go any faster than him." Then God said, "You will pass many of them."

God then showed me a Christmas tree. Jesus was at the top, and He said, "That is a type of my body. When you get born again, there are a lot of you, but the closer you get to being like Jesus, the less of you there will be." I then told God the tree should be upside down where there are more like Jesus.

Ezekiel 34:10 RSV

Thus says the Lord GOD, Behold, I am against the shepherds; and I will require my sheep at their hand, and put a stop to their feeding the sheep; no longer shall the shepherds feed themselves. I will rescue my sheep from their mouths, that they may not be food for them.

I put this in this letter, but I believe God said put the whole chapter of Ezekiel 34 in it. Ezekiel 34 is for the Moses ministers of today who are not going into what God had promised them because they would not glorify God.

Ezekiel 34:2-4 RSV
Israel's False Shepherds

The word of the LORD came to me: 2 "Son of man, prophesy against the shepherds of Israel, prophesy, and say to them, even to the shepherds, Thus says the Lord GOD: Ho, shepherds of Israel who have been feeding yourselves! Should not shepherds feed the sheep? 3 You eat the fat, you clothe yourselves with the wool, you slaughter the fatlings; but you do not feed the sheep. 4 The weak you have not strengthened, the sick you have not healed, the crippled you have not bound up, the strayed you have not brought back, the lost you have not sought, and with force and harshness you have ruled them.

That's what is happening today from most pulpits. Do you think God is not going to do something to these shepherds of today? When the ministers are not building up the saints, which is God's primary purpose for the ministers, the sheep will still be children, tossed to and fro and carried about with every wind of doctrine, by the cunning of men, by their craftiness in deceitful wiles. Most today want more sheep but they are not building up the sheep they already have, to do the ministry God has anointed them to do. I call it abortion; they want to get people to confess Jesus and pray a prayer. So, the seed is planted in them but then they do nothing to help them become a child of God.

John 1:12 KJV

But as many as received him, to them gave he power to become the sons of God, even to them that believe on his name:

John 1:12 AMP

But to as many as did receive and welcome Him, He gave the right [the authority, the privilege] to become children of God, that is, to those who believe in (adhere to, trust in, and rely on) His name.

You see, they are like a seed in a womb but then aborted and not built up by the ministers who were given to the body as a gift to build them up so they could become the sons of God. The ministers are neglecting their duty for God for the saints. Most people teach, just ask Him to come in your heart and you will be saved or be a child of God. This scripture says when you do that (believe in His name) you are given power to become children of God.

This scripture does not say that you are automatically a child of God as some people say. So, at the time you receive Jesus and believe in His name, you are then given the power to become a child of God. There is more to being a child or son of God then simply believing in His name.

This scripture shows you that once saved always saved is a lie, or when they say just except Jesus by praying this prayer and you will go to heaven. I had been born again for 3 years and went to New York City to Teen Challenge to take a course on street ministry for four weeks. God used me a lot, but when we were on the streets ministering, these Baptist people would tell people just pray this prayer and you will go to heaven. I am not saying all Baptist do this because I really do not know what they teach, but these Baptists were teaching that. When they would get done with the people, God would give me words of knowledge for healings or what they needed prayer for. When the Baptist saw God healing and blessing the people, they got mad and complained about me to the leadership. Thank God, the leaders were open to the Spirit.

I ended up teaching the Teen challenge course in the Good Samaritan Mission in

Charleston South, Carolina under pastor Albert J Salmon Jr. I had ministered on the street there one day and several people got healed. I told Albert God wanted me to teach there. He said he did not know anything about that. That Friday, he called me and said that his Teen Challenge teacher quit, and asked, would I teach it.

The first day in class, this was in 1987, I told the men there, who some of them were the ones who got healed when I ministered there, that I was a Joshua not a Moses. When I said that their jaws dropped. I asked, "What's up?" They all said the previous teacher said he had to leave because God told him he was a Moses and God was bringing a Joshua teacher to them.

I do not teach people to look to mc but to God. Just like a tennis coach takes the students on the court to learn, I take people on the ministry field and let them experience hands on teaching, even in church services. I do not let them observe like most ministers today. They show how God uses them to minister instead of teaching the saints how to minister. They'd rather get the recognition of God using them, than building up the saints to do the work of the ministry. You do not build the saints up by always having them watch you minister but instead getting them on the court to hit balls.

They can flow in the Spirit just as you do. You are not special, but a gift to teach them how to be led of the Spirit and flow in the gifts. I do not know of any instructor who is always showing but never letting the students get hand on experience. If that's you, you're in trouble with God. Repent and start asking God how to function as a gift to His saints and build them up.

Ephesians 4:14 RSV

So that we may no longer be children, tossed to and fro and carried about with every wind of doctrine, by the cunning of men, by their craftiness in deceitful wiles.

The shepherd feeding the sheep means they lead them to pasture. It is stated again below by God "I will feed them with good pasture". That's what God means when He says, "feed my sheep."

Ezekiel 34:5-9 RSV

So they were scattered, because there was no shepherd; and they became food for all the wild beasts. 6 My sheep were scattered, they wandered over all the mountains and on every high hill; my sheep were scattered over all the face of the earth, with none to search or seek for them. 7 "Therefore, you shepherds, hear the word of the LORD: 8 As I live, says the Lord GOD, because my sheep have become a prey, and my sheep have become food for all the wild beasts, since there was no shepherd; and because my shepherds have not searched for my sheep, but the shepherds have fed themselves, and have not fed my sheep;

9 therefore, you shepherds, hear the word of the LORD: 10 Thus says the Lord GOD, Behold, I am against the shepherds; and I will require my sheep at their hand, and put a stop to their feeding the sheep; no longer shall the shepherds feed themselves. I will rescue my sheep from their mouths, that they may not be food for them.

Most ministers today say we need to get more souls saved. However, God is saying, you're supposed to be building my sheep up but are scattering them and so on. God is not happy at all with what is going on today. Just like when He had the above written by Ezekiel. I want to repeat what I said before, the only thing you as a child of God need to be taught is how to be taught by the Holy Spirit. If the ministers do not or are not taught by the Spirit of God, they cannot teach you how to be taught by God. So just let God home school you. He is your shepherd.

God, the True Shepherd
Ezekiel 34:11-15

"For thus says the Lord GOD: Behold, I, I myself will search for my sheep, and will seek them out. 12 As a shepherd seeks out his flock when some of his sheep have been scattered abroad, so will I seek out my sheep; and I will rescue them from all places where they have been scattered on a day of clouds and thick darkness. 13 And I will bring them out from the

peoples, and gather them from the countries, and will bring them into their own land; and I will feed them on the mountains of Israel, by the fountains, and in all the inhabited places of the country. 14 I will feed them with good pasture, and upon the mountain heights of Israel shall be their pasture; there they shall lie down in good grazing land, and on fat pasture they shall feed on the mountains of Israel. 15 I myself will be the shepherd of my sheep, and I will make them lie down, says the Lord GOD.

As per example of verse 14 and 15, God is showing that the role of a shepherd in feeding the sheep is to bring them to good pasture which means being taught by the Spirit. God wants to be your shepherd. To let Him be your shepherd, all you must do is be led and taught by the Holy Spirit. Those who are led by the

Spirit of God are the Sons of God. All of creation is awaiting the manifestation of The Sons of God. So, you could say all of creation is awaiting the ministers to build up the saints.

Ezekiel 34:16

I will seek the lost, and I will bring back the strayed, and I will bind up the crippled, and I will strengthen the weak, and the fat and the strong I will watch over; I will feed them in justice.

When God says I will seek the lost in this passage, I believe in this Joshua generation, He is saying those led by the Spirit will be one with Him in seeking the lost. Just like Jesus said, "I and the Father are one", so those who are led by the Spirit are also one with the Father in seeking the lost.

Ezekiel 34:17-31

"As for you, my flock, thus says the Lord GOD: Behold, I judge between sheep and sheep, rams and he-goats. 18 Is it not enough for you to feed on the good pasture, that you must tread down with your feet the rest of your pasture; and to drink of clear water, that you must foul the rest with your feet?

19 And must my sheep eat what you have trodden with your feet, and drink what you have fouled with your feet? 20 "Therefore, thus says the Lord GOD to them: Behold, I, I myself will judge between the fat sheep and the lean sheep. 21 Because you push with side and shoulder, and thrust at all the weak with your horns, till you have scattered them abroad, 22 I will save my flock, they shall no longer be a prey; and I will judge between sheep and sheep. 23 And I will set up over them one shepherd, my servant David, and he shall feed them: he shall feed them and be their shepherd. 24 And I, the LORD, will be their God, and my servant David shall be prince among them; I, the LORD, have spoken.

25 "I will make with them a covenant of peace and banish wild beasts from the land, so that they may dwell securely in the wilderness and sleep in the woods. 26 And I will make them and the places round about my hill a blessing; and I will send down the showers in their season; they shall be showers of blessing.

27 And the trees of the field shall yield their fruit, and the earth shall yield its increase, and they shall be secure in their land; and they shall know that I am the LORD, when I break the bars of their yoke, and deliver them from

the hand of those who enslaved them. 28 They shall no more be a prey to the nations, nor shall the beasts of the land devour them; they shall dwell securely, and none shall make them afraid. 29 And I will provide for them prosperous plantations so that they shall no more be consumed with hunger in the land, and no longer suffer the reproach of the nations.

30 And they shall know that I, the LORD their God, am with them, and that they, the house of Israel, are my people, says the Lord GOD. 31 And you are my sheep, the sheep of my pasture, and I am your God, says the Lord GOD."

John 10:14-18 ESV

I am the good shepherd. I know my own and my own know me, 15 just as the Father knows me and I know the Father; and I lay *down my life for the sheep. 16 And I have other sheep that are not of this fold. I must bring them also, and they will listen to my voice. So there will be one flock, one shepherd. 17 For this reason the Father loves me, because I lay down my life that I may take it up again. 18 No one takes it from me, but I lay it down of my own accord. I have authority to lay it down, and I have authority to take it up again. This charge I have received from my Father."*

Are you laying down your life so the Father will love you? Are you heeding Jesus's voice? Whose voice are you listening to? Whose words are you obeying? Are you being led by words interpreted by a person or the Holy Spirit?

Romans 2:28-29 ESV

For no one is a Jew who is merely one outwardly, nor is circumcision outward and physical. 29 But a Jew is one inwardly, and circumcision is a matter of the heart, by the Spirit, not by the letter. His praise is not from man but from God.

2 Corinthians 3:4-6 ESV

Such is the confidence that we have through Christ toward God. 5 Not that we are sufficient in ourselves to claim anything as coming from us, but our sufficiency is from God, 6 who has made us sufficient to be ministers of a new covenant, not of the letter but of the Spirit. For the letter kills, but the Spirit gives life.

Are you being killed by the written code? Or are you getting life by the Spirit? The shield of faith is what God is saying to you. The fiery darts are words other than what God is saying to you that you're hearing and believing. See Ephesians 6:10.

Jesus said in
John 10:26-28 ESV

"but you do not believe because you are not among my sheep. 27 My sheep hear my voice, and I know them, and they follow me. 28 I give them eternal life, and they will never perish, and no one will snatch them out of my hand."

Are you being taught to hear God's voice which is your evidence that you are one of God's sheep and He will give you eternal life? Wait a minute some would say, "I was told all I had to do was pray a prayer, and I would be saved and go to heaven. I was never told there was so much more"

You see, a shepherd leads the sheep to green pastures. When Jesus said feed my sheep in those days it meant pasture them.

Gentiles Hear the Good News
Acts 10:34-35 RSV

So Peter opened his mouth and said: "Truly I understand that God shows no partiality, 35 but in every nation anyone who fears him and does what is right is acceptable to him.

Do you fear the Lord? Are you doing right? How do you know what is right and acceptable? Jesus said my sheep hear my voice and do not follow another. Ask God to help you hear Jesus' voice if you're not hearing it, so that you can do what is right and acceptable by being led by the Spirit. He never said listen and obey a fleshly leader. Submitting to a leader God did not tell you to submit to is like marrying a woman or man God did not tell you to marry. Now a days it is like a man marrying a man and a woman marrying a woman. You will never produce what God had in store for you if you stay married to them, same as you submitting to a leader God did not tell you to submit to. You will never bear the fruit He wants you to because you are not connected to Jesus the true vine.

Slaves and Masters
Ephesians 6:5-9 ESV

Slaves, be obedient to those who are your earthly masters, with fear and trembling, in singleness of heart, as to Christ; 6 not in the way of eye-service, as men-pleasers, but as servants of Christ, doing the will of God from the heart, 7 rendering service with a good will as to the Lord and not to men, 8 knowing that whatever good any one does, he will receive the same again from the Lord, whether he is a slave or free. 9 Masters, do the same to them, and forbear threatening, knowing that he who is both their Master and yours is in heaven, and that there is no partiality with him.

This is why we should hear from God on what to do in all situations and be led by the Spirit. Handle each situation as God would have you handle it, and not follow your flesh that wants you to please man.

Sing the old song by Joseph M Scriven:

What a friend we have in Jesus, All our sins and griefs to bear! What a privilege to carry Everything to God in prayer! Oh, what peace we often forfeit, Oh, what needless pain we bear, All because we do not carry Everything to God in prayer!

Have we trials and temptations? Is there trouble anywhere? We should never be discouraged— Take it to the Lord in prayer. Can we find a friend so faithful, Who will all our sorrows share? Jesus knows our every weakness; Take it to the Lord in prayer.

Are we weak and heavy-laden, Cumbered with a load of care? Precious Savior, still our refuge— Take it to the Lord in prayer. Do thy friends despise, forsake thee? Take it to the Lord in prayer! In His arms He'll take and shield thee, Thou wilt find a solace there.

Blessed Savior, Thou hast promised Thou wilt all our burdens bear; May we ever, Lord, be bringing All to Thee in earnest prayer. Soon in glory bright, unclouded, There will be no need for prayer— Rapture, praise, and endless worship Will be our sweet portion there.

I was going to stop here, but God wants me to add one more thing.

The Judgment of the Nations
Matthew 25:31-37 RSV

"When the Son of man comes in his glory, and all the angels with him, then he will sit on his glorious throne. 32 Before him will be

gathered all the nations, and he will separate them one from another as a shepherd separates the sheep from the goats, 33 and he will place the sheep at his right hand, but the goats at the left. 34 Then the King will say to those at his right hand, 'Come, O blessed of my Father, inherit the kingdom prepared for you from the foundation of the world;

35 for I was hungry and you gave me food, I was thirsty and you gave me drink, I was a stranger and you welcomed me, 36 I was naked and you clothed me, I was sick and you visited me, I was in prison and you came to me.' 37 Then the righteous will answer him, 'Lord, when did we see thee hungry and feed thee, or thirsty and give thee drink?

When I read verse 37 as a baby Christian 40 years ago, I asked God, "Wait, these sheep were your people, why did they not know they were supposed to do these things?" God spoke to me and said, "My ministers are not telling them." Has any minister you have been listening to told you about the judgment day coming? Are they telling you what you are going to be judged for? Are they telling you to do these things?

I just had a thought. I watched Fiddler on the Roof, and they observed the sabbath in their homes. At that time, the Passover was in each home and the people were called a congregation.

Exodus 12:5-6 AMP

Your lamb or young goat shall be [perfect] without blemish or bodily defect, a male a year old; you may take it from the sheep or from the goats. 6You shall keep it until the fourteenth day of the same month, then the whole assembly of the congregation of Israel is to slaughter it at twilight.

Exodus 12:6 AMP

You shall keep it until the fourteenth day of the same month, then the whole assembly of the congregation of Israel is to slaughter it at twilight.

Literally between the two evenings, that is, between sunset and nightfall (likely 6:00-7:20 p.m.) each household was to slaughter its own lamb or goat.

Exodus 12:7 AMP

Moreover, they shall take some of the blood and put it on the two doorposts and on the lintel [above the door] of the houses in which they eat it.

The Bible is referring to the people in their homes as the whole assembly of the congregation of Israel. So, congregation does not always mean in the Bible, people all in one building. The Hebrew meaning of congregation here means "the Hebrew people collectively as a holy community."

What God is saying to me is that we as a congregation of sons of God, the Joshua generation, should be doing Matthew 25 from our homes not a church group but collectively as a holy community led by God's instructions just as they collectively did the Passover from God's instructions through Moses. If they did not obey, they would lose a child.

How much more is God expecting us to obey Matthew 25 after having the Bible as evidence of the way God handles things? How much more does He require of us having given us a better covenant? What will you suffer by not obeying Matthew 25? Now you can see why God is upset with church leaders telling you to give money, that God has entrusted to you, where they want you to give instead of God and His word telling you where to give. The teaching of the tithe today under the new covenant, is not from God regardless of what some may say. If you believe the tithe is of God for you to give to a church, you are not hearing His voice or reading and studying the word and letting the Spirit bring you life. The word is killing you. You are also depriving those in Matthew 25 from receiving what God wants you to give them or minister to them. Read Matthew 25 again. Whatever you do unto them, you are doing to Jesus. So, if you are not doing or giving to them what God wants, you are depriving Jesus, who died for you, and you "appreciate" it so much that you will not minister to Him. Read where you are going for not ministering to Jesus.

Matthew 25:38-44 ESV

And *when did we see thee a stranger and welcome thee, or naked and clothe thee?*

39 And when did we see thee sick or in prison and visit thee?' 40 And the King will answer them, 'Truly, I say to you, as you did it to one of the least of these my brethren, you did it to me.' 41 Then he will say to those at his left hand, 'Depart from me, you cursed, into the eternal fire prepared for the devil and his angels;

42 for I was hungry and you gave me no food, I was thirsty and you gave me no drink, 43 I was a stranger and you did not welcome me, naked and you did not clothe me, sick and in prison and you did not visit me.' 44 Then they also will answer, 'Lord, when did we see thee hungry or thirsty or a stranger or naked or sick or in prison, and did not minister to thee?'

The goats use the word minister here. The ministers are a gift from Jesus to build you up for the work of the ministry. Are they doing that for you? Are you being equipped to know the voice of Jesus so that as you walk about your daily life, you will hear Him when He speaks to you? He may ask you to pray for someone, give money, give a word of knowledge, or simply lend a helping hand to a person in need.

Are you being taught how to minister to those around you as Holy Spirit leads you every day?

This is also called sowing to the Spirit, and be assured, you will reap from the Spirit. You are laying up treasures in Heaven. Jesus said, "If you give a feast, invite those that can't invite you back.... You will be repaid at the resurrection of the just." Luke 14:12-14 When you are led by the Holy Spirit and do what He says, you are sowing seeds, performing righteous deeds, and obeying the commands of Jesus your Shepherd. You will receive an eternal reward.

Ephesians 4:11-16 ESV

And he gave the apostles, the prophets, the evangelists, the shepherds and teachers, 12 to equip the saints for the work of ministry, for building up the body of Christ, 13 until we all attain to the unity of the faith and of the knowledge of the Son of God, to mature manhood, to the measure of the stature of the fullness of Christ 14 so that we may no longer be children, tossed to and fro by the waves and carried about by every wind of doctrine, by human cunning, by craftiness in deceitful schemes. 15 Rather, speaking the truth in love, we are to grow up in every way into him who is the head, into Christ, 16 from whom the whole body, joined and held together by every joint with which it is equipped, when each part is working properly, makes the body grow so that it builds itself up in love.

God told me a few years ago, the ministers who are not building up the saints for what God has anointed the saints to do for God are anti-Christ. Then, God told me the ministers who are telling the saints what to believe for, are also anti-Christ because God wants them to do exceedingly abundantly above what they can ask or think. The minsters have them focused on what they can ask or think (which is well beneath what God intends for the saints). Then God told me, these ministers are going to hell.

Understand that anti-Christ means against Christ. Christ means the anointing that God puts on an individual to fulfill God's purpose in their life for them for God. Ministers that are not building up (or equipping) the saints for the work of the ministry (specifically the ministry/work that God has anointed them for to build up the body), are in effect, working against God.

There's so much more I could teach on the leadership in the churches that is out of order.

Go to 1 Corinthians 14. The whole chapter talks about what should be going on when we come together. Again, back then they gathered in houses. They didn't have buildings.

1 Corinthians says let the prophets speak two or three. Then it says judge what is being said for God is not the author of confusion. So, if two or three prophets are not speaking and what is being said is not judged, there will be confusion.

I have never seen two or three prophets speak and then what's being said judged in a service, and that is why there is so much confusion in the churches. That is not happening in any church I know of. Is it happening in yours? If you bring a word to the leaders, you are rejected and will not be there long. There's so much more I could teach on about what is not going on in church services, that's not of God, and what God is not allowed to do in the services because the leadership is not being led by God. I may address it in another letter. The Bible says *those that are led by the Spirit of God are the sons of God.*

If every service at your church is the same and the people are not being taught to prophecy and be led by the Spirit as 1 Corinthians 14 says, you all may prophesy one by one, then the leaders are not being led by the Spirit and are not building you up to be led by God.

Like I said there's much more, but if you're not being taught to be led by the Spirit, get out of there. As I said before, let God homeschool you. The Bible says you have need that no man teacheth you, but the Holy Spirit will. If the pastor is constantly keeping the focus of the "flock" on what the pastor wants them to believe for and accomplish for him and never encouraging the flock to hear what God, Himself, is saying specifically to them, that pastor is working against Christ and you in this matter on behalf of the saints.

By not telling them God can or expecting God to do through themselves exceedingly abundantly above what they can ask or think by the power at work within them allowing the people to be stretched in their walk with God to move beyond the flesh and fully into the Spirit, they are keeping the people back from what God wants them to be or do for God.

If the pastor or head minister is not teaching the "flock" to cultivate a relationship with God where each of them can have confidence in knowing the voice of the true Shepherd for themselves and keeping them to where they always need the pastor in order to "hear God", that pastor is anti-Christ, working against the will and purpose for each believer. Jesus died so we can know God our Father and come into the Holy of Holies as individuals, to have our own personal relationship with Jesus, to know, hear, and follow His voice only. Christ is the head of the church. If you have a pastor as a head and Jesus as your head, you have two heads. No one can serve two masters. In other words, you can't satisfy two heads.

All ministers are gifts from Jesus to build you up, not be your head. To build you up to listen to the head and only the head, who is Jesus. You're only supposed to have one head, one shepherd. Most ministers are keeping you from knowing Christ as your head because they teach you, they are your head, you need to listen to them, you need to do what they tell you, you need to join their denomination, you need to not miss church, Bible study, or anything else their church is doing. They are not teaching you to be led by the Spirit, that Christ is your head, the Holy Spirit is your teacher, and that you don't need a man to teach you. That's what Jesus said. It is in the word, but they are not teaching you that because they want to control you and have you follow their denomination or their church or them, not God or Jesus the one who died for you.

Shepherds do not pick the grass and feed it to the sheep, they take the sheep to green plush pastures where they can safely graze and get properly nourished. Ministers are to lead the people to God's pasture where they can receive His food, be filled, and then walk out their purpose as they are led by His Spirit. We are to be a body, unified in the Spirit and one with

God, working together to fulfill the purpose of the Body of Christ. Each person understanding what part of the body of Christ they are, their function in and for the body, and submitting to the leading of the Holy Spirit will accomplish this. This will never happen following a man or denomination instead of being led by the Spirit of God.

Titus 1:16 ESV

They claim to know God, but by their actions they deny him. They are detestable, disobedient and unfit for doing anything good.

James 1:22-25 ESV

But be doers of the word, and not hearers only, deceiving yourselves. 23 For if anyone is a hearer of the word and not a doer, he is like a man who looks intently at his natural face in a mirror. 24 For he looks at himself and goes away and at once forgets what he was like.

25 But the one who looks into the perfect law, the law of liberty, and perseveres, being no hearer who forgets but a doer who acts, he will be blessed in his doing.

Apostle Andrew Giannelli

A messenger of God

CONTACT INFORMATION FOR
APOSTLE ANDREW GIANNELLI
Email:odm@homesc.com

Apostle Andy and Family

Charleston, South Carolina